Angelica Lee

LIFE ON THE GAME

a true story

Michael Terence Publishing

This edition first published in paperback by
Michael Terence Publishing in 2022
www.mtp.agency

Copyright © 2022 Angelica Lee

Angelica Lee has asserted the right to be identified as
the author of this work in accordance with the
Copyright, Designs and Patents Act 1988

ISBN 9781800943865

No part of this publication may be reproduced, stored
in a retrieval system, or transmitted, in any form or
by any means, electronic, mechanical, photocopying,
recording or otherwise, without the prior
permission of the publisher

Cover image
courtesy of Angelica Lee

Cover design
Copyright © 2022 Michael Terence Publishing

Contents

Introduction 1

1: How I Started and Where It All Began 3

2: My First Call 9

3: My Techniques 23

4: Variety and Opportunity 35

5: Parties and Families 45

6: Questions and Answers 51

7: What Have I Achieved? 61

Introduction

I'm 25 years old and my adult chat line name is Angelica. I've worked in the adult sex industry since the age of 18. I've escorted, run my own massage parlour, provided over-the-phone adult chat services, photographed, edited and sold my adult content; I've written for an adult magazine and now I'm writing this book.

Sex work takes many forms, from street walking, escorting, webcamming, pole dancing, stripping, featuring in adult pornography and providing over-the-phone sex chat to paying customers.

The purpose of this book is to educate, to provide an understanding and genuine insight into the world of a British sex worker, and just some of the encounters we face.

This is a true story with no embellishment. The situations written about are real, the people are real; the statistics are authentic and based on first-hand research conducted by me, Angelica, the author of this book.

Only some names and details have been changed, to protect the identities of the individuals involved.

Adult phone sex has been a booming business since as far back as the 1980s, providing over-the-phone companionship to millions of paying customers. At the age of 18, I commenced my work as a phone sex operator. This is my story.

I:
How I Started and Where It All Began

One month after my 18th birthday, I started work as an escort. I was young, not streetwise and began working for two pimps. I assumed that by working for these men, who later turned out to be drug dealers and people traffickers, I'd be safe and have an opportunity to make good money. I soon discovered how much I hated working for them. I didn't like the drugs I was exposed to, nor their misogynistic attitudes and the way they told me to say and do things I definitely didn't agree with nor want. Deep down I knew I could do things a whole lot better, so eventually, we parted company.

Turning the key in the gold metal lock and pushing open the door, I stepped inside, finally home after a long day. It was a dark October evening and I craved nothing more than a large mug of steaming hot chocolate and a biscuit. As I removed my shoes, the feeling of the thick, white carpet beneath my aching feet felt simply blissful. Glancing around, seeing the television and lights off, it was clear that no one else was home. I made my way to the kitchen turning on the lights and heating as I passed through the hallway, then flicked the switch at the base of the silver kettle.

"Gosh, what a day it has been!" I said out loud, taking a deep breath before carefully pulling a tight hairband from my hair.

I set out a mug then turned the metallic silver kitchen blind and briefly inspected the back garden. I couldn't help noticing how depressing it looked at this time of year. Soon the kettle boiled and I found myself searching for the hot chocolate sachets,

"Oh, no such luck, I will have to make it a tea then," I muttered quietly to myself while closing the cupboard door in my mother's outdated kitchen.

Pouring the hot water into the mug and watching while the tea bag floated to the top, then pouring in the milk, thoughts began to rush through my mind of the day's events. Once the tea was ready, I made my way into the lounge and set the mug down on a round, retro-style coffee table. I threw myself down on my mother's two-seater sofa and instantly felt the soft cushions under my back, relieving the tension and stress from my muscles. Minutes later, I reached for the remote control, switching on the telly and turning to ITV News, wondering what had been happening in the world, as I heard the familiar theme tune begin to play.

Sitting myself up straight, I placed the mug to my lips and took a small sip of tea that had slightly cooled down, then I pulled out my mobile phone. I had not checked it in hours and now, connected to WIFI, I received a crazy number of notifications. Scrolling down I noticed a job advert, it didn't stand out particularly and there were only very vague details about the job role, but I was well able to read between the lines.

I sent a direct message to the young, attractive woman who had placed the advert:

'Hi, my name is Angelica, I'm 18 and interested in the ad you've posted. Please could I have more information regarding the job role? Many thanks, Angelica Lee.'

Once the message was sent, I forgot about it almost immediately and settled down to watch the evening news.

A whole week went by and I hadn't given the message a second thought. Then standing in a queue at a warm bakery, with the smell of cakes and delicious pastries filling the air, I suddenly got a reply and we started texting:

'Hi, Angelica I am Sarah. I understand you want more information about the job role?'

'Yes, that's correct.'

'Are you 18 and over?'

'Yes.'

'Do you have a mobile phone?'

'Yes.'

'Look can I just be really honest.'

'Is this a Sex Chat line Job?'

'Lol, Yes it is, is that not what you're looking for?'

'No, it's fine I'm in the industry anyway so over the phone work would be no big deal.'

'Look, Angelica, I'll give you my manager's number and you can call her, her name is Janice she has been running the business for years.'

'Cheers that will be great'

'If you have any issues, please don't hesitate to contact me.'

'That's fine thank you Sarah'

Looking around the bakery, chuckling to myself, I thought well this should be fun.

"Next please!" shouted the slim, middle-aged lady at the till, in a high-pitched voice.

"Next please, indeed!" I smirked while slipping my phone into my leather bag as I approached the glass counter.

Later that evening, I went home and received a call from a mature-sounding woman.

"Hello dear, my name is Janice. I understand that you are interested in working for our service?"

"Hi, yes I'm Angelica and I am interested."

"So, can I start by asking, have you ever worked in the industry before?"

"No, never done over-the-phone work."

"Ok, so I have your email address. I'm going to send you an email and you can go through the steps, confirm age, give me bank details for you to get paid and you should be ready to go. Can I ask, dear, is your real name Angelica?"

"No, sorry it's my escorting name."

"Oh, ok that's fine dear; most girls use cover names and we are fine with that as well."

"Fantastic," I replied. "So, I'll fill out the paperwork and send it back to you, Janice."

"Great, thank you love."

I completed all the paperwork and by the next day, I was up and running. I felt 100% confident in my abilities. I have great charisma, I'm fun and very, very imaginative, so I knew this was something I could do. I just couldn't wait for my first call because despite having been paid to have physical sex, I had no idea what working on a sex chat line would bring.

2:
My First Call

"Hi, how can I help you?" I said in a soft, slow, seductive voice.

"Hi, I'm Mark. So, what are you wearing?"

"I'm wearing absolutely nothing."

And with that, the phone went down; the client hung up. Many girls in the industry would take offence at this. However, it's not about what you are saying to these clients, it's the tone of your voice that can turn them on.

It's important when providing a service, that all call operators make themselves sound as seductive as possible. I've had numerous clients tell me that after hearing a girl's voice just for a second, they know they are either attracted or not. On one occasion, a regular caller of mine described how he called the lines and a girl with what sounded like a Birmingham accent picked up.

"Hi, it's Jodie," she said.

"She sounded as boring as a doorknob," he said. "So, I'm glad I got through to you, Angelica."

My phone rang again. I wondered who it would be this time.

"Hi, how can I help you?"

"It's Mark, I think we spoke a moment ago?"

"Oh yes, I thought you hung up?" I said in a playful voice.

"No sorry, you just instantly made me cum as I was already horny."

"Oh, you naughty, naughty, naughty man. Mmmmmmm, now let's see if I can make you cum all over me?"

In an instant, I could hear Mark masturbating his throbbing cock.

"Yeah, that's right, can I cum all over your arse, tits and face?"

"Of course," I replied. "Let's not forget to cum in my mouth."

Our session lasted for over an hour; by then we had anal sex, I had gagged multiple times on his penis, swallowed cum, had cum all over my face and lay sideways, taking a hard pounding in the pussy hole. We both felt exhausted by the end of it and I did all this from the comfort of my own home, slippers on, hot cup of tea beside me, TV on subtitles and yes, I got paid for it.

The strange thing is, after doing an over-the-phone session, I personally never thought about it again. It was as if nothing had just happened and I had been relaxing with slippers, fire and TV on the whole time.

Moments later the phone rang and I heard a whispering voice.

"Hi, I'm Rod."

"Hi, Rod and what can I do for you today?"

"Well, I have a foot fetish. What toenail colours are you wearing?"

"Bold red; do you like bold red?"

His voice deepened as he slowly asked:

"What shoe size do you take?"

"I'm size 8, slender feet, with soft soles. Is that ok for you Rod?"

"That's perfect, just perfect," and suddenly he hung up.

What surprised me the most was that when working the lines, some callers were happy to talk for less than 5 minutes. However, as I continued and became more experienced, I would ask them questions, keep them talking and soon I appeared to have my very own little fan club who would talk to no one else but me.

When first working on the phone lines, especially on my very first day, I felt somewhat deflated. Many callers instantly hung up within a second of hearing my voice; no matter how appealing I made myself sound, they still hung up. I phoned the service and explained that I had a couple of good calls but some of the others were just hanging up. Calmly and soothingly, Janice reassured me.

"It's all because your new, regular callers who have never heard your voice before, often hang up before plucking up the courage to call back, nothing personal to you."

Callers, Love Bombing

In the world of an adult phone chat operator, we understand that when having an intense session and suddenly a client hangs up, this often means that the client has reached their climax. During the day-to-day job of a phone chat operator, we could often be called multiple times a day by the same client; there is nothing unusual about this and it can feel rather flattering. However, if you sense that a client is becoming rather obsessive about you or is almost love bombing you and you feel, uncomfortable, it's important to be open and honest with the service and request that they block this caller. Hanging up when they call can be another alternative.

Hanging up on callers who you feel are obsessive about you should be ok. As with many services, their call can be diverted to another phone operator so there's nothing to worry about. However, this doesn't mean that you won't find yourself in trouble with the service that you work for, so please ask them for advice on what to do, regarding these callers.

During my time as a phone sex operator, I would sometimes - but not often - have regular callers who would tell me:

"I love you; we will be together one day. I want to marry you."

If this happens, it's nothing to worry about. You should feel satisfied that you are doing a good job in evoking such positive emotions from a caller.

Information Check List

When working on an adult sex phone line, often people fail to understand that you don't have to use your personal phone, the one that friends, family and associates call you on. Additionally, it's important to understand that you don't use your personal phone number for paying clients to contact you. For some phone line companies, you can earn more by working from your landline. However, a cover number must be provided by the phone chat company.

Always check out the company you are thinking of signing up to; this can be done simply by searching out the company reviews using the internet. Depending on the reviews, you must make the right decision and if something doesn't feel right, as with anything in life, don't join a service.

The checklist:

Must be 18 and over.

Check out phone line company reviews, think and make a decision based on the reviews.

All adult chat companies should provide each operator with a cover number. However, it's important to ensure that it's provided in advance and you should ask before committing to work for a service.

Establish a persona.

Establish an acting name.

Buy a small, pay-as-you-go, mobile phone for as little as £10.00. Call someone you know from it, to establish the clarity of the line.

Ensure you always have the volume turned up as loud as possible and your phone is on vibrate, during the times that you are working.

Good acting skills are essential; be ready to slip into your persona immediately.

Examples of names: Naughty Nicki; Sexy Sarah; Dirty Doreen. These are just little examples of names to use when working on the lines. However, you can create your own and of course, you can use your real, birth name if you wish; it's strictly up to you.

If you choose to establish the persona of a Dominatrix, for example, Sadistic Sadie, Dominant Delilah would be ideal, due to the nature of your chosen persona.

Choose a persona you are comfortable with. Some examples of what callers are looking for:

Girl Next Door

Lonely Housewife

Woman Home Alone

Mistress

Dominatrix

Slave Giving

Slave Receiving

Naughty Neighbour

House Maid

Office Worker

Escort

It's important to understand that as a phone chat operator, you don't have to be constrained to only one persona; in fact, you can have as many as you like and be creative.

The Lonely-Hearts Callers

Working on the phone lines, the majority of callers I spoke to wanted a sexual service and I was more than happy to provide them with it. However, some just needed to talk. For instance, one explained that he was elderly and had divorced his wife years ago. We spoke extensively and he explained that he had casual friends to talk to, however, he craved female company. We had a long conversation and by the end of it, I could sense that his mood had lifted.

Another caller disclosed that he worked in a bakery and after many years of marriage, he divorced his wife. As with similar callers, he simply wanted someone to talk to. He described himself as a black male from the Midlands and told me all about his family and life as a baker. At the end of many of our long chats, he appeared less lonely and depressed, as if he had, had his fix. It's amazing how a conversation lasting less than an hour, can have an impact on a person's emotional wellbeing.

The Smoker

During my time in the adult sex industry, it was common to come across a wide range of unimaginable fetishes, including smoking.

Ring, Ring, Ring.

"Hello, who is this?"

"It's Gary."

"Hi, Gary and what can I do for you today?"

He paused.

"I have a smoking fetish and I want to hear you light up a cigarette and smoke."

Reaching into my bag, I pulled out my packet of Silk Cut and a lighter. Holding the phone to the lighter, so the client could hear me light up, I began to smoke the cigarette.

"Oh, yes that fantastic, oh yes, oh yes, you're making me cum. I was in prison for 15 years and I used to dream about birds like you. That's fine, all I want you to do is smoke for me."

I continued and after the session had come to an end, I composed myself and decided out of curiosity to have a look at this caller's social media profile. For whatever reason, I chose to look at his friends' list. I could not believe my eyes! The caller turned out to be a close friend of my mother's ex-partner. Thank God we never met, the word "awkward" shouted out loud in my head. It didn't matter how many phone sessions I'd have with this caller or how much time I'd spend on the phone with him, we never really talked about sex; it was strictly smoking, nothing more, nothing less. As I soon came to realise, human beings are strange characters.

Funny, crazy and totally bizarre Kaylee, the possible Lesbian

Ring, ring, ring.

"Hello, how can I help you?"

"Hi, I'm Kaylee."

"Hi Kaylee and what can I do for you today?"

"Well, I'm on my own at the moment and I can't walk."

"Aww, that's terrible," I replied, completely confused as to where the heck this was going.

"Look, as I can't walk, I struggle and find it hard to wipe my bum."

What on earth? I thought to myself, rolling my eyes.

"See, the thing is, as I'm unable to wipe my bum, I have a couple of female friends who have to do it for me; am I a lesbian?"

By now, many phone operators would have put the phone down. But I was hooked, wondering what on earth this caller would say next.

"No, not if you have a disability and you're unable to walk," I replied.

"But I like it when they come around and wipe my bum."

"So, you enjoy it then?"

"Yeah."

"Maybe you really are a lesbian, then?"

"Oh, no!" she shrieked and the phone went down.

I never heard from the caller again.

The Knicker Sniffer

Now I was born into a Roman Catholic family, so going to church is a normal occurrence. On this one particular day, I said my prayers, lit some beautiful candles and asked for forgiveness for my sins. Strolling back through the churchyard, I pulled out my phone and just then it rang. Scanning the area, to make sure no one was near, I proceeded to answer the call.

"Hello, this is Angelica, how can I help?"

"Hi, I've got an underwear fetish. I'm sniffing a pair of white lace knickers at the moment."

"Aww well, so long as it keeps your wife happy, I say do it."

"No, no, no. They're not my wife's, I've never been married."

"Oh, go on. Are they the neighbour's?" I laughed.

"No, I'm at work."

"At work?" I interrupted.

"Yeah, I'm a plumber, the woman of the house has gone out."

I could not stop laughing.

"What if you get caught out?"

"Oh, well I like the risk of getting caught."

The phone went down and the moral of the story is never leave a workman in your house alone.

The Lipstick Lovely

Ring, Ring, Ring.

"Hello, my name is Angelica and what can I do for you?"

"Hi, I'm Malcolm."

"Well, hello Malcolm, what can I do for you at this late hour?"

"I'm in the lounge, my wife is in bed and I'm wearing my wife's lipstick."

"Awww, do you enjoy wearing her lipstick?"

"Yes, and sometimes I wear her shoes."

"You like to cross-dress as they call it?"

"I do," he whispered. "She knows nothing about it. Well, I'd better go now, I need to go to bed."

"Well, make sure you wipe the lipstick off first, darling."

The caller then hung up.

The Shocker

"Hello, my name is Angelica, how can I help you today?"

"Hello, my name is Raj and I'm into toilet slaves."

"Ok, fantastic."

"Yeah, can you pretend to shit in my mouth please and let me eat your shit? Could you also pretend to watch me while I eat your shit, Angelica?"

Suddenly the whole world came to a standstill but it's money and business.

"Of course."

Instantly, I began making loud noises as if I was actually defecating into his mouth. Once the session finished, I knew then I had totally lost my innocence.

How Patronizing

Personally, there's nothing that angers me more, than being patronized over sex work. As soon as someone begins to patronize me, I feel like an overflowing pot of boiling water, like a massive vat, ready to explode.

People who discover how I make money often say:

"No. No, really? That's a shame, you seem like such a nice girl."

When people say this, I can't help myself and respond:

"Well, of course, I'm a nice girl, so I bloody should be."

People often look at me in astonishment but the fact remains, in my opinion, I am a nice girl. So, the question is simply this, do only nasty girls work in the sex industry?

People look flustered and say:

"No, no, that's not what I mean."

However, they never truly explain what it is they do mean by their reactions.

At the age of 18, when I first started in the industry, I would often become slightly offended and stop the conversation. However, as I've got older, I feel I've matured from the wide-eyed, baby-faced sex worker I once was and now hold my counsel and simply try to educate people. Ultimately, it's about learning to manage my own emotions rather than storming off huffing and puffing. Learning to remain calm in order to educate people is crucial in the sex industry because if you appear approachable, people will often ask questions; then I can answer them as thoroughly as possible and society ends up better educated on the subject.

3:
My Techniques

Disclaimer:
These are the techniques of Angelica Lee and this is not to advise any person to do the same.

When people call on the phone, you never know what the nature of their request will be; each one is completely different, there really is no general example. They could be anything from a doctor to the local postman. It's important for all call handlers or operators to be as flexible as possible, because if you are only comfortable with one particular fantasy, then you are likely to earn less money. So, it's important to have as many techniques as possible ready to use during each session.

Callers asking to be spanked or slapped is a regular request. If they asked to be spanked, I would often slap my thigh or arm to create the sound of skin being slapped.

Many callers appear to enjoy urination. I used to run a tap and place the phone near the running water. This appeared to create the sound of urination.

When having a deep and heavy session, if the caller asked me to turn over, I would slightly move in my chair, making enough noise to play into the caller's fantasy that I was actually turning over for them.

Some techniques I used would be to ping my bra strap if requested to wear stockings.

Using my nails, I would carefully claw my trouser legs, to create the effect of putting on underwear or undressing.

In some cases, I would lightly tap a hard counter or even a wall to create a light thud, during sessions of humping.

Mouth noises, smacking my lips together and making various other mouth noises can be a very valuable tool when working on phone lines, so if you wish to do so, it's strictly up to you.

Breaking Ignorance and Gender Imbalance

I have found it's extremely common for individuals, at some stage in their lives, to wonder what it would be like to be a sex worker. There are a number of reasons why anyone would even contemplate working in the sex industry, from wanting to make more money, gaining a more flexible work-life balance, enjoying sex and liking the idea of making a living out of it, even just down to simple experimentation. In my opinion, there is nothing wrong or abnormal with having these desires.

The general opinion seems to be that people who work in the sex industry are poorly educated and can't find any other job. Another common myth is that sex workers are only in the industry to feed a drug or alcohol addiction and again, have little or no education to speak of.

In my wide experience of working in the sex industry, I know that many workers, male and female, are often university college students, or working professionals, supplementing their income alongside the day job.

Statistics

Approximately 1 in 25 students in the UK has engaged in some form of sex work

85% of students engaging in sex work have often felt unsupported by their educational establishments.

Sexual Abuse

During my time working in the sex industry, many people have asked me:

"Were you sexually abused as a child?" Or, "What was your upbringing like?"

The sad truth is yes, unfortunately, I did experience sexual abuse as a child, not only once but twice. The first time was when I was a very small infant, so I remember very little about it. Then again as a child of 10, by a female babysitter whom I trusted implicitly. After the assault, I felt thrown into a world of total confusion; the perpetrator was a married woman! She was also a mother I had always thought highly of. I just couldn't believe it. At first, I was scared that maybe I had misinterpreted the situation; if so, I would have hated to see someone in serious trouble. The scary thing was that the woman who sexually assaulted me was not only a babysitter, she was a foster carer, mother and childminder. This haunts me as I dread to think of all of the children she must have abused in her care, as she had unlimited access to vulnerable children, including some with serious cognitive learning difficulties and that really makes my blood run cold. She lived in a big house, surrounded by greenery, with chickens, rabbits and a small dog, an almost idyllic home for children.

I struggled with what had happened in the early days. Months went by and, I attempted to tell my private tutor, whom I had known for over a year. We were working at the round wooden table in our kitchen at home. To my right sat Mabel, my tutor, a big built woman with lots of silver jewellery; she had once been a 70s hippie and often talked about her travels as a young woman to far-flung parts of the world. Mabel was a mother of two, a genuinely lovely lady and I got on well with her.

Plucking up the courage, I placed my pen down decisively. Mabel looked at me over the top of her coffee mug in anticipation of what I was going to do next. I took a deep breath.

"Mabel, can I ask you something?"

"Yes, dear."

Seeing I had her undivided attention, I ploughed on.

"If someone touches your breasts, is it not right?"

Mabel's eyes widened as she slammed her mug of coffee down onto the wooden kitchen table, almost breaking the mug and replied in her booming voice:

"Of course, it's not right!"

I was frozen in shock. Oh no, I better say no more, I thought to myself.

Fear started to kick in as a result of Mabel's reaction and the reality of the situation began to dawn on me. Due to the perpetrator's position in the community, the fact that she was a woman, married and a mother would make it almost impossible for anyone to believe that she would molest a child.

Mabel looked me hard in the eyes.

"Has someone done this to you?" she asked.

Shaking my head, I denied it.

"No, no, not at all," I said, then quickly changed the subject.

When I was 7, sadly, we moved to a small, suburban town, where the population could only be described as racist, backward and in my opinion, frankly inbred. As with many children who had already endured a tough life, I fell into minor trouble with the law and did not achieve anything at primary school. My dilemma was simply this: what chance did a town's outsider and local nuisance have of being believed when accusing a well-known pillar of the local community of sexual assault? If I did report her actions, I knew it would bring serious repercussions on me or my mother. I'd either be framed by police or sectioned, pumped full of medication and confined to a mental institution if I had spoken out.

Even at the tender age of 11, somewhere deep down I had an inner sense that I'd be stepping into some very dark water if I tried to bring down a woman so highly regarded by the community, especially in such a racist, backward, suburban town where locals referred to themselves as 'The Family'.

This became clear at a meeting with my mother and my then head teacher. As my mother and I sat opposite her, the woman leaned across the desk towards us in a very sinister way, removing her glasses and in a menacing tone said:

"What you have to understand, Miss Lee, is we are a *Family* in these parts!"

With a chilling smile, she relaxed back in her chair.

Following my near disclosure, Mabel and I never talked about my suspicious question again. Mabel never even mentioned it to my mother. Fortunately, I managed to compartmentalize the situation, I had no choice; by 16, I finished school and in October 2012 my mother and I left the small town never to look back.

Anyone reading this might be wondering what has any of this got to do with sex work or adult sex chat? I feel it's important to include these details because this book is designed to educate people and part of that education is to help people understand how perpetrators can seem so normal on the surface; just because someone is a woman, married and busy helping the community, it doesn't mean she isn't harbouring dark secrets or can't be a paedophile.

I've never fully got over the sexual abuse but you learn to live with what has happened. Thanks to my mother, brother, managers and a conversation with the Rape Crisis charity, I've managed to come to terms with what happened to me. Following my disclosure, my mother proved kind and supportive and advised me to go to the police to make an official statement regarding the incident. As much as I wanted to see the perpetrator face legal punishment, I knew that it was too late. No DNA evidence existed; it was a case of my word against hers.

When I discussed it with my mother, we both had to, unfortunately, accept the reality that with no DNA, no recordings of any sort and my word against hers, it was unlikely to even reach the threshold of going to court, unless she actually admitted her vile perverted actions. I knew my chances of getting justice were slim, to non-existent.

I've never had to appear in court for any reason. However, if it meant giving evidence or testifying against a paedophile, I definitely would step up, to keep people safe and achieve justice for the victims.

A few days after telling my mother about the abuse, I woke up to a bright July morning and of course, the first thing that came to mind was my disclosure. So, like millions of other people on first waking up, I looked at my mobile phone. Where was the perpetrator now? I wondered. So, from the comfort of my bed, I chose to make some enquiries. Within less than an hour, I found myself dropping my Galaxy phone in utter shock; I had to read and re-read the news before finally yelling out to my mother.

"Mum! Mum! Mum!"

"What's going on?" she shouted back at me from her bedroom.

"You know that old bitch who molested me?"

"Yes?"

"She's dead."

I heard a loud gasp, followed by the sound of my mother jumping out of her large, king-size bed. Then she ran through the landing, bursting into my bedroom, with bare feet, nightdress and bleached blonde hair looking like she had been pulled through a hedge backwards.

"How do you know? How do you know?" she repeated,

Rolling my eyes and in a calm voice, I explained.

"Mum, it's called the internet! People can find things out easily these days."

Covering her mouth with her left hand, we looked at each other in shock. Slowly moving her hand away from her face, she asked:

"Awwww, I wonder what it was that killed her?"

"Well, I don't know. But according to what it says here, she died 8 years ago, the year I left school."

Looking at me, my mother's eyes darkened.

"Oh right, well I hope someone comes along and throws dog shit all over her grave then!" she said in a ruthless and menacing tone.

"Sounds like not a bad idea," I replied with a hint of sarcasm.

Of course, I had no intention of doing any such thing, I was just relieved she was gone. Although the news that she had died did come as a massive shock, it still felt like the best form of justice. People might think, I never got justice because I never took her to court but I felt a huge weight had been lifted from my shoulders, knowing she could never touch or harm anyone else ever again. I could now breathe, knowing I'd never have to go to the police, sit through interviews with an assigned officer, agree to video interviews where I'd describe the crime; it was over.

The most upsetting part of her obituary was where it described her as: "A loving mother and foster carer to lots of lucky children."

I wanted to be sick and I felt angry reading that.

People do ask me if it's because of the sexual abuse that I work in the sex industry. I honestly don't feel that connection in myself, and throughout my many sexual encounters, I have never thought about what happened and it never stopped me from enjoying sex or providing a great service. Sadly, many sex workers have suffered sexual abuse just like me and I have met some who say they do sex work as a way of exercising control over the crimes committed against them. Personally, I just do a job that I really like.

Gender discrimination

Unfortunately, throughout my time in the sex industry, I have often come across gender discrimination. Female sex workers are thought about and treated less favourably than their male counterparts, who are often admired for what they do and this is where the gender imbalance occurs.

Male sex workers are often described as playboys or players and are generally viewed in a more positive light. People imagine a 6ft tall, handsome man, with a glowing complexion, beautiful eyes and muscular body. However, the image of a female sex worker attracts such insults as slags, sluts and whores. They are often thought of as addicts and if they have children, society seems to view them as unfit to be a parent. In many cases, Social Services or Child Protection Services become involved with families where a parent or parents are sex workers.

From my personal experience of working in the sex industry, transgender sex workers attract the most criticism and disregard and so do the clients who use their services. Throughout my life as a sex worker, I have been present when people outside of the sex industry have made derogatory comments, for example referring to transgender workers as "weirdos" and "freaks".

Unfortunately, many misguided people make references to Thailand, suggesting that all transgender sex workers originate from there and other parts of Asia, when in reality this is simply untrue; transgender sex workers come from a wide variety of countries, ethnic backgrounds, cultures, creeds and religions.

Why Some People Use Sexual Services

1. The reason why some clients use my services is because they feel that using a sex worker will enable them to develop and build on their sexual skills, as well as help to overcome any issues they have regarding sex.

2. Many of my clients have told me that they feel pressure sexually and especially when having their first sexual encounter. One client told me when he had his first sexual encounter, he felt like an actor featuring in a film. He also told me he had a deep desire to impress the woman but all he really wanted was just to be his true self. This client also described how the encounter could result in either no relationship or turn out to be the start of a real romance and he always felt nervous about the outcome.

3. When having sex with clients, many of them have issues not only with physical conditions but also can struggle to reach an erection or achieve an erection at all. However, many of my clients have described feeling that they were not being judged and I immediately put them at their ease.

4:
Variety and Opportunity

Having sex with people is not the only thing you do as a sex worker. The thing is I'm also a fully qualified Swedish Massage Therapist who ran what's known as a Happy Ending Service, also referred to - and as I prefer to call it - a Rub and Tug Service. I first heard the term Rub and Tug while spending time in America with some relatives. I'd never heard of it before but since then I have definitely considered it my personal favourite. Rub and Tug - love it!

At times clients would pay to simply sit and talk about their issues while I would sit wearing sexy lingerie with one hand on their cock. One client wanted to smell my buttocks while holding his throbbing cock in hand and masturbating incessantly.

Another client who always claimed to be well off would lay me down on the massage table after sex, then holding his cock in his hands, draw spots of sperm on my 21-year-old face. The strangest things can happen.

As an industry girl buying underwear, not only sexually but personally, there was a local sex shop I'd frequent to buy items such as lingerie and lubricant. On one occasion I noticed a lady working there who I'd never seen before. We got talking and soon the discussion moved to my work. This woman revealed to me that she too had worked in the sex industry, in fact, she was a former Dominatrix. Apparently, in many UK sex stores, people working in them are not permitted to have previously worked or be currently working in the industry. Personally, I find this shocking and in my opinion yet another form of discrimination.

On one occasion when I was in the store this woman beckoned me into a small side room. As I walked in and glanced to the left, I couldn't believe my eyes.

"Do you like my art?" she asked, proudly smiling at me.

Stuck to a long, duck egg blue wall were pornographic cut-outs of men and women in different sexual positions; pictures of men's heads stuck on women's scantily-clad bodies, women in positions giving men blow jobs, and in a number of other sexual positions, lesbian sex gay sex. She was an ordinary-looking woman, tall, well-built, she was certainly no Picasso but her imagination was clearly incredible. The one thing I have often found is that people in the sex industry can be some of the nicest and most creative individuals.

"Wow, that's something you sure don't see every day," I replied, smiling back at her.

"Yes, I get bored occasionally, so I like to come out here and get creative."

Working as a Sex Worker I have to admit has opened many doors for me. I've had offers to participate in the Adult Film Industry, Adult Modelling. I have had Sugar Daddies approach me, however, personally I don't trust them because I think it's important for all human beings to make their own money and take their place in the world, not rely on a stranger to fund them.

From the age of five, I was raised by a hardworking, single parent who owned her own home, drove a car, raised me and held down a job as a social worker, so I knew that it was possible for someone to achieve, even with no one to turn to. Growing up my mother and I only had each other, so I had to be a survivor. I was born to an abusive father and a hostile maternal family. One aunt made it clear to my mother:

"Now you live near us, there is nothing we can do for you," then put the phone down.

It was tough growing up. Despite my mother's family living locally, on the occasions that she was ill, they'd never come up to our house to check if we were ok. They wouldn't call or even text. So, I'd often spend long periods of time alone completely unsupervised having to maintain a house, cook, clean do the shopping and check on my sick mother, through days and nights when I was alone and I knew no one would come.

On one occasion, my mother underwent an operation that left her immobilized for three months, during which time her family never made contact. When she started to regain some mobility, we decided to go shopping. We bought so much food that we had to push the shopping trolley up the hill, as my mother was still unable to drive due to her operation. While pushing the heavy trolley up the hill, with my mother walking along beside me on crutches, suddenly the trolley appeared to hit a stone, and the whole thing overturned with food falling out all over the street. I felt so sorry for my mother that day as she cried her heart out.

No matter how ill she was, she'd often rub my face and tell me how blessed she was to have me. It felt so good and a real confidence booster. I always seem to thrive on praise; in life, you only need one person to believe in you, encourage and advise you and this is where my strength comes from. My mother was the third eldest, a stunning daughter of 1960's Irish immigrant parents who first came to Sheffield, then Birmingham before finally settling down in Kent where they raised seven children. According to all accounts from my mother and other family members, it became clear that she was often singled out and bullied by her own immediate family growing up. My mother had to become a survivor after such a seemingly brutal upbringing.

During my own childhood and despite the horror stories I'd hear about my mother's childhood, I tried hard to get along with her family. However, we never got on, so at sixteen I decided to throw in the towel and have as little physical contact with them as humanly possible. I felt this was the only way forward. There's a famous saying: "Know when to throw the towel in". I've never been a quitter but there are some circumstances in life when you need to know when to throw in the towel and if you are being lied about and verbally abused then it's time, despite how emotionally challenging it may seem. As with any issue in life, why remain in a place of unhappiness?

In life I'd rather be as independent as possible, emotionally and financially independent and no one's sugar baby. People fail to realise that life in itself is simply temporary and everything that goes with it, from jobs to relationships, friendships, marriages, homes and tragically even the ones we love; it's all just temporary and everything is just a phase. This is why it's important for people to establish their own lives and forge their own careers because at any time the plug could be pulled on a lavish lifestyle if you are reliant on someone else to provide it for you. The fact that anyone needs to buy the affections of another, through money, luxury holidays and expensive clothes, in my opinion, makes me think a sugar daddy or mummy suffers from the ultimate in low self-esteem or enjoys exerting financial power and control over another.

Like so many sex workers, I have been involved in the Adult Modelling side of the industry. My first professional Glamour Modelling shoot took place in Essex and it was fun and professional. Walking into a modern, white reception room, I was met by Mark, the agency owner. He was a tall, handsome, former model with 20 years' modelling experience. He was so good looking with beautiful blue eyes and I still can't believe that he was not world famous because he looked like a film star.

A week went by since the shoot and at 7 am on a cold morning I found myself standing at a local train station waiting to be picked up by Max, a partner in the modelling agency. My phone rang, it was Mark, the handsome head of the agency.

"Hiya, Angelica, my friend will be with you in a minute."

"Hiya, ok great I'm just waiting."

Just then a massive BMW pulled up with a dapper-looking man at the wheel, who rolled down the passenger window.

"Angelica!" he shouted, flashing a smile.

"Hi," I said, stepping forward. "I have to go, Mark, he's here."

"Ok, great."

I stepped into a massive, cream leather seated BMW; it was beautiful and immediately Max and I started talking as if we had known each other for years. Of course, stepping into a car with a total stranger is never advisable and the amount of risk I have put myself in is…well totally off the planet. Thankfully, I'm able to read human behaviour quite well. I didn't feel safe but strangely I didn't feel unsafe either but I remained watchful as we drove through London. Lighting up cigarettes, we chatted about all sorts of things, then I was informed we would be picking up a couple of other models.

Driving through London we stopped on a residential street and coming out of a house was a model that I had passed in the agent's office. She was a tall, slim Hungarian who appeared rather self-important. We then picked up another model who in conversation referred to Max as "Baby, Baby" in every other sentence. Looking at Max out the corner of my eye, I felt he didn't like it but I knew he was just playing along with it.

Finally, we arrived at the UK's largest swingers and lifestyle club. After stepping out of the car and glancing around at a stunning wooded area, I and the other models found ourselves being led down a path to a small, yet cosey caravan. When we opened the door and climbed inside, we found a 21-year-old woman called Toni, wearing only underwear as she applied her make-up while listening to Alaska Thunderfuck. I couldn't help thinking how young she looked. There was also 35-year-old Kay, doing her make up. I had never met these women but they made me feel welcome. Slipping into fishnet stockings, a black mini skirt, black heels and a basque top, I didn't know what to expect. Stepping out of the caravan, we were all led to The Dungeon. I'm not into BDSM so I'd never been in a Dungeon before. Inside, I received a pleasant surprise.

"I know you," I said to the handsome photographer.

"Do you?" he replied, looking up at me wide-eyed. It was Richard, one of the Glamour industry's leading photographers and one of the best.

The dungeon was painted red, with a red carpet, mirrors and a black steel cage in the corner, with a 7ft wooden X-shaped instrument with handcuffs and ankle cuffs. I've never understood the world of BDSM; it all seemed like pure torture. Standing in the dungeon, I and the models were divided up and sent off with different photographers to different parts of the resort.

Looking back, I can hardly believe that I took off with a total stranger and went to a Sex Resort. At the time I knew there would be risks involved but I've always taken risks, enjoying the rush is satisfying…well I think so. Following my shoot at the resort, there was a party that evening, of course, I had fun, dancing like crazy around a pole, drinking like a fish and had to be carried out at the end of the night… naughty, naughty.

Following my day of the shoot, I chose to do what I love, writing about my experiences. Putting pen to paper I wrote about my experience and later I received a call alerting me to my first publication, in an X-rated magazine. I later went on to become a columnist for a Fashion, Photography magazine.

I love writing, I always have. At the age of about 8 or 9, while sitting on the floor watching telly, my mother walked into the lounge.

"Look, what I bought you," she said.

I could see writing books in plastic packaging; it was a writing kit. I have dyslexia so I always found literacy a struggle and wasn't too sure if I'd genuinely like the gift. I opened it anyway.

"Thank you, mum," I said, looking up with a beaming smile.

Picking up the pencil and looking around the lounge intensely, I just couldn't think what to write. Little did I know this would probably be my very first writer's block. And then it came to me, why not write a story using my imagination? I started writing and could hardly stop; my mother didn't see me all weekend, I was so busy putting pen to paper.

5:
Parties and Families

When people think that models and celebrities often attend raging parties, that's actually very true. Once involved in modelling, I was invited to different parties, especially around London's famous Mayfair area. While attending one of these London parties, I noticed Richard a well-known industry photographer, taking pictures and directing people where to stand. Glancing up at me he said,

"Angelica, would you like to come to a shoot next Wednesday?"

"Of course," I replied.

I couldn't wait as the shoot was held in one of London's most infamous strip clubs, long associated with rich clients and classy ladies. I had been to the club before and it's where I met my model, and 'Extra' friend Sally. Sally and I had been talking for months online before finally agreeing to meet.

I saw her, standing on the side of the street, hair tied up tightly, leopard print fur coat, black leather skirt and choker necklace.

"Hiya, Angelica," she said with a smile leaning forward for a kiss on the cheek.

We started talking and soon made our way to the strip club. As we stepped inside, we were stopped by a 6ft blonde model dressed in a pale pink outfit.

"Are your names on the guestlist?"

"Of course, my name is Angelica."

She ticked my name on her list and looking at me with her big blue eyes, the tall attractive blonde stepped aside. Another attractive blonde, standing behind her, leant forward and handed Sally and me a glass of Champagne each.

As we walked through, we saw lots of people we recognised and were pulled up for photos. Photos over, we made our way into the main room. Looking straight ahead I saw a stunning girl of about 23 dancing around a pole centre stage. People were transfixed by her. We sat at a round table with a perfect view of the gorgeous performer.

Sally and I talked as if we had known each other for years. We had a fantastic night and ended up in the early hours of the morning, sitting in a small club in Marylebone.

On the day of the shoot, I stood outside a black metal door, just me and a slim Thai model. The door opened and I saw Richard the industry photographer, dressed in casual jeans and a white top.

"Hi, girls," he said and led us downstairs, via the back entrance of the strip club.

We found ourselves in a long dressing room, with black metal lockers, mirrors and makeup stations. I'd never done a shoot at this club before but I was looking forward to it. After slipping into underwear and doing my make-up, I emerged onto the stage. Richard was busy taking his shots and I noticed Marshal, the club's General Manager dressed in an expensive business suit, sitting at the back of the club observing the shoot.

Once it was over, I emerged out of the back of the club into a cold November morning around 10.30 and I decided not to go home immediately but to stay in London and have breakfast in the bustling capital.

Sitting in a cafe, with a cup of tea and toast I began to reflect on the morning. Some women would be feeling on top of the world, a shoot in a high-end London location but I like to try and remain as grounded as possible. Looking out of the window on a busy London morning, a great sense of pride came over me. I'm proud of my city, I'm proud of the work I do, however as I say, I prefer to feel grounded and not swan around like some models who after a few shoots seem to think they are world-famous. Outside the café window, I saw hundreds of students on their way to university. As much as I had enjoyed the shoot, the geeky side of me would much rather have been sitting in a classroom learning some highly academic subject, but at this point that was definitely not happening, in fact, I was studying for my Diploma 2 in Health and Social Care.

That evening I got home and showed my mum the pictures, she couldn't believe it. Later, she admitted how shocking she found it that my breasts were out. Sometimes people say to me are you crazy to go off to some strip club and have pictures like that taken of you? But then I've always been fearless in many ways.

Sometimes in life, it's a whole army of people that you need; sometimes it's just that one person who loves and supports you unconditionally. My Mum and I often talk about my sex work. When I started at 18, she was worried, embarrassed and deeply ashamed. My sex work had a profound impact on her and even affected relationships with other family members and friends. Coming from a massive Irish Catholic family, a career in the Adult Sex Trade isn't a recommended way of making a living and my family have frowned upon my work, even estranging themselves from us. But my Mum has learned so much from being a single mother, raising kids on her own and having to act as both parents, so in her opinion, as she says,

"Who cares what my family think of you? You're my precious girl, so fuck 'em, who are they anyway?"

With my mother being a single parent, going on holiday on our own was just something that we did. When I was about 5 years old, she decided to take us both away for Christmas and fly to Portugal. The holiday was generally going well so we decided to go out on Christmas Day. Driving around the Portuguese town and finding our way through the cobbled backstreets, we saw a bar, with flashing neon lights.

"This place looks amazing," said my mother. "I wonder if they let children in?" She looked at me then out of the car window for a minute. "Well, let's have a look."

She parked the hire car and as we stepped out, we could hear music playing and the lights were flashing brightly. We walked inside and saw a young bartender wearing a black shirt, pulling drinks and chatting to a male customer at the bar. As we reached the bar, the atmosphere started to change, men were staring at us with their mouths wide open in shock.

"Happy new year!" said my mother, flashing a beaming smile.

The bartender looked totally uncomfortable. We

ordered two drinks and sat down, glancing around the bar.

"Gosh, there's a lot of men in here," she said.

The whole bar continued to stare at us. I loved the flashing lights, the music I didn't even notice people watching us, like any kid I felt excited, it was Christmas, I was on holiday and in this fabulous bar with flashing lights and music. Placing her drink down, my mother looked at me,

"Angelica, I think we'd better go."

"But why, Mummy?" I said looking up at her.

Now my Mum has never been one of the most diplomatic people. Leaning forward, she said,

"We are in a brothel, sweetheart."

"But Mummy, what's a brothel?"

Putting down our drinks, we made our way out of the bar, with me still shouting,

"Mummy, what is a brothel?" in my posh London accent.

She didn't answer and we got into the car to drive back to the hotel,

"Let's go," she said. "We'll see if there's a restaurant open."

My mother never told me what a brothel was or what it meant until I was about ten years old. I remembered our trip to that Portuguese bar at Christmas and thought, Oh, my gosh!

6:
Questions and Answers

Here are just some of the questions I am asked when talking about how I make money, by people who do not work in the sex industry.

"Do you like what you do?"

"Yes."

"Do you do drugs?"

"No."

"Do you have any addictions or mental health issues?"

"No."

"Have you ever had an STD?" (sexually transmitted disease)

"Definitely not."

"Do you feel embarrassed, ashamed or guilty about working in the adult sex industry?"

"No, never, I love what I do and anticipating the next caller's conversation. Each day is so different and the conversations can really vary. Why should I be ashamed of what I do? I'm not hurting anyone."

"Are your parents, siblings or other family members aware of what you do?"

"Yeah, my family knows, as do close friends. However, family are not as open-minded or accepting of how the money is made."

"Do you work in the industry by choice or do you feel that there is no alternative? Will you ever stop working in the adult sex industry?"

"I love what I do and work in the industry by choice. I have also worked in jobs outside of the sex industry and even co-workers know what I do. No, I enjoy working in the industry so I probably won't exit it just yet."

"Do you ever feel dirty or shallow?"

"No, never have. Money is money."

"Would you allow your children to work in the industry, once they are of legal age?"

"Yes, if they wanted to, money is money. I would obviously advise them of the dangers of meeting clients and that if found out, they could lose their jobs, so it's not advisable.

Discrimination

I have always faced discrimination from the day I started right up to now. I've received many abusive communications, calling me a variety of vicious names.

Turning up for a London party, some models and I were standing outside a Mayfair nightclub when a large car pulled up and a group of women began shouting:

"You're a whore!" then drove off.

Despite insults being hurled at us by a group of complete strangers, nothing and no one was going to stop our fun. By the end of the night, we'd all enjoyed a wonderful evening and nothing got in our way.

Another regular occurrence that we as working girls or industry girls as we sometimes call ourselves, experience is to be on the receiving end of penis pictures. Hundreds of men deem it acceptable to send abusive communications and images of their private parts.

I have often bravely asked what they hope to achieve by this but have never received a definitive answer. So, I have never gained a full insight or understanding into their mindsets. Only on very few occasions have the men responded, by telling me:

"Well, I thought that's probably what you would want to see. You look horny and you are an escort, so I thought that's what you wanted."

"No, it's not acceptable and please don't contact me again," and then I simply block them.

It feels like an unconscious bias, that if a woman looks or presents herself a certain way, or is a sex worker, automatically men assume that we all want to see obscene images of their privates. I believe that men who intentionally send women, or anyone, penis pictures without being asked to do so, are often dangerous and no different to men who indecently expose themselves to innocent bystanders. In my view, it's just another form of indecent exposure.

Banks have also been accused of discriminating against sex workers by cancelling their bank accounts and advising them to go somewhere else when applying for mortgages.

Without a Moral Compass?

When people know what I do for money, they often come to an automatic conclusion. Many assume that I am an addict, poorly educated and promiscuous. These are false stereotypes and I'm seriously none of those things. The reality is that I have never suffered from drug or alcohol addictions. I have worked in mainstream jobs and even done volunteer work in my local community, and no, I don't walk the streets wearing a mini-skirt and fishnet tights; that's another cliché out there in society concerning sex workers.

I never enjoyed servicing married men because in my view, if you're married why not divorce your wife and then meet someone new? When I was 5 years old, my mother discovered that my father was having an extramarital affair with an American woman he met online in an internet chatroom back in 1996, around the time she was pregnant with me.

My father was a computer geek and would spend hours conducting his online affair, even pretending to go on a business trip to Birmingham when in reality he flew to the USA to meet his middle-aged, online companion, not to mention the fact he was also being serviced by London male and female sex workers. A nurse once told my mother:

"If your husband isn't having sex with you, he's getting his end away somewhere else."

I agree with her.

Now, I'm in Trouble

As many people are aware, as well as working in the sex industry, I have had many mainstream jobs, mostly within the care sector. I've worked with different client groups, even becoming 'Employee of the Month'. Throughout my career in the care sector, there is one particular Nursing Home that I really enjoyed working in. The management was amazing, the staff great…Well some of them, anyway and the service users were always well cared for and appeared to be happy.

Originally, when I first started at this particular nursing home, it was run by an older lady in her mid to late 60s, a knowledgeable Nurse with decades of experience. After a long time running the home, she decided to step down and promote Leah, the younger 35-year-old, rosy-cheeked, ambitious deputy. Leah was a fantastic nurse, tomboyish in her manner and style.

After a while, a senior care worker by the name of Queenie finally took on the role of the new deputy. I had worked with Queenie directly and every shift you always felt safe when Queenie was in charge, so I was delighted when I discovered that she was the new deputy. Queenie was beautiful, calm and strong and we all got on really well.

During the COVID-19 pandemic, all care homes had to have weekly swabbing for all staff members. From the cooks to cleaners, management and carers we all had to be swabbed or would not be allowed to work. On this particular day, I turned up, not to work a shift but to be swabbed. It was my day off but earlier that morning I received a call from Leah, asking me to see management.

I wondered what was going on. If management calls you in, it's often not a good sign. I had my swab and all was clear. I found myself waiting for half an hour to be called into the office, all sorts of thoughts ran through my mind. No problems or issues had arisen the day before; I got on well with the team -most of them; my quality of care was always considered over and above fantastic and my documentation was always up to date. I just couldn't understand it.

Queenie walked into the testing room. I looked up at her but she didn't even give me a second glance, just turned on her heel and walked out. What the heck was going on? I felt confused and said to a senior care worker:

"I'm going to walk out in a moment if I'm not called in."

Then I heard Leah's voice ask loudly from her office:

"Is Angelica out there, Queenie?"

Queenie appeared in the doorway, wearing a beautiful blouse, black trousers and strappy shoes. I honestly couldn't read her expression; I didn't know what was going on, everything was quiet. As I walked into the office, Leah glanced up from behind her computer she was typing at on her desk.

"Could you close the door please, Angelica?"

That was it; I knew I was going to lose my job, but what for? I just couldn't think. I had gone through everything in my mind and I couldn't find anything they could say I had done wrong.

"Could you take a seat, please?" continued Leah.

I sat down in the comfortable navy-blue chair, staring back at Queenie and Leah.

"Do you want to start then, Queenie?" said Leah, giving her a reassuring look.

"Ok," said Queenie. "So, we were aware you took part in a reality show."

"Ok, yes I did."

"But after the show, we looked up your name and it brought us through to a social media page."

I knew right then I'd been found out.

"So, Angelica," Queenie smiled at me. "It seems care work is not your only occupation, is it?"

"No, it's not," I said in an honest tone.

"See, the thing is Angelica, Leah and I have spent most of the morning watching your Porn in the office. We have seen your tits, fanny, arse and everything else."

Looking up from her computer, Leah, turned directly to face me.

"We even saw the tattoo on your arse, Angelica, while you featured in a free view clip, naked and hanging out the washing."

What could I say?

"Oh, yeah, it was me, I'm sorry. At least you can't say you've had a boring morning!"

I laughed, we all laughed and couldn't stop. That was the beauty of working under these managers, they were both fantastic and the best management I've ever had. The general acceptance was great.

"Well, on the upside," I said in a calm voice and leaning forward, "at least if I need a reference one day, you can say you know me so well, even intimately."

We all started laughing again.

"Look, Angelica, I am going to have to ask you to take down the content from social media. You're a care worker, a professional; please, if a family member came to visit a relative and recognized you, it could be all over the papers and we can't have that."

Reluctantly, I had to remove the content and make things harder for people to see. Sometime later, the clinical lead manager and I talked about my antics. She was a brilliant manager and a stunning, Jewish lady and told me that she and her husband previously owned a tiny convenience store and often a local sex worker by the name of Luscious Leyla would come in to buy drinks. The amazing thing was that despite how I made money, never once did these 3 managers guilt-trip me and that's why I loved working for them. When people discover that my managers found my content, they're often quite shocked. One person asked, "Angelica, how could you possibly have had the front to go to work each day, knowing your managers had seen you naked? I mean, you have to face them and sit in serious meetings with them, doesn't it feel humiliating?" Of course, I'd prefer management not to have seen my content as I like to keep sex work separate from my mainstream job. However, what sex worker would survive in the industry if they had an issue with clients seeing them naked or watching their content? It simply wouldn't be possible. It's common for many adult content creators to upload free views as a way of enticing clients, so the chance of someone you might know and trust finding your content is highly likely.

I was delighted not to be sacked or asked to resign over my content or sex work. This brings a tear to my eye, butterflies in my stomach, a lump in my throat and makes me feel somewhat… emotional. This is what I want to see and the future I want everyone to work towards, acceptance. When management found my content, I felt this provided them with a chance to ask direct and frank questions about my work. Then, by continuing to work in the Care profession I believe I demonstrated that besides my work in the sex industry, I was more than capable of working in a professional environment outside of it. I felt a duty to break down barriers and negative stereotypes of sex workers and prove to my managers that I'm a regular person, not a stupid, naughty little girl as I have been called in the past. What enrages me is how we live in these times of equal opportunities. The UK has Human Rights laws in place to stop discrimination, yet society still has a negative and often ignorant attitude toward sex workers. I'd love to see sex workers gain the right to continue working in mainstream jobs without the fear of losing that job hanging over them, which has happened to some. Sex workers should be entitled to live where they want and make money from working at home, without a landlord evicting them because of it. Personally, I suspect that even if I live to a grand old age, I won't see a world and society where many positive changes have been brought about to empower sex workers.

7:
What Have I Achieved?

As a result of working in the sex industry, I have met some amazing, inspiring people. At 21, I was featured in an adult magazine owned by two London businessmen whom I first met at the age of 19. I had been on a reality TV show, become a blogger, a model, had my own beauty column and worked as a journalist. I attended some great parties and met some amazing celebrities. Needless to say, the industry has opened many doors for me that I would never have experienced otherwise.

What about when you meet your maker?

People often look shocked when they find out that I believe in God or have any faith at all. Catholicism and Buddhism both interest me greatly. Society finds it hard to understand when looking at any human life; it's as if we each have our own circle, starting with our names, educational status, jobs, foods we like, habits, sexuality, fetishes, dress sense, mannerisms, political leanings, hobbies, interests, favourite animals, favourite weather, religion and more. Because a person is employed in the sex industry, it doesn't tell you everything about them, so no one should be surprised to find out we have a faith.

I was once told that outside many temples in India, you will see sex workers, before or after their work, praying to God or Gods for their sins. We are all put on this earth for a reason so I feel it's important to accomplish as many of our goals as possible. Take every good opportunity and try to be the best person possible; give your fears to Jesus so that one day when you die, you can look God in the eye and tell Him what you did with the life He gave you.

---

*Available worldwide from
Amazon and all good bookstores*

www.mtp.agency

www.facebook.com/mtp.agency

@mtp_agency

www.ingramcontent.com/pod-product-compliance
Lightning Source LLC
LaVergne TN
LVHW041542060526
838200LV00037B/1108